THE PRODIGAL DAUGHTER

A Maundy Thursday
Reconciliation Service

BY MAXINE DUDLEY

C.S.S. Publishing Co., Inc.
Lima, Ohio

THE PRODIGAL DAUGHTER

Scripture quotations are from the New Revised Standard Version of the Bible, copyright 1989 by the Division of Christian Education of the National Council of the Churches of Christ in the USA. Used by permission.

9310 / ISBN **978-1-55673-563-9**

For Mac,
Adela
and little Dell

Introduction

Although all are precious in God's eyes, many see only their imperfections when they consider repentance. They fail to see the God that loves them and calls them personally to himself.

In February of 1991 while working as reconciliation team leader for a women's retreat, I searched the scriptures for verses which depicted Jesus forgiving women. I had a strong desire to construct a religious drama where worshipers could see a loving Jesus, a loving Father. I hoped that such a drama in the reconciliation service would eliminate any of the retreatant's fears to return to God.

After much study, I wrote *The Prodigal Daughter*, which is philosophically similar to *The Prodigal Son*. In *The Prodigal Daughter* the love of the Father is seen in the symbol of the mother. But unlike the prodigal son who directly repents to the father, the lost daughter asks Jesus for forgiveness in prayer and then returns home to the mother (Father). This was introduced to signify that forgiveness is gained through Jesus.

The Prodigal Daughter is appropriate for any reconciliation service, but is especially relevant during Lent, the season of spiritual reawakening. As a religious service, it dramatizes the Father's love for us and his ardent longing for us to return when we stray. Since this is a story of relationships, the characters of the drama speak personally to each of the faithful.

A church can implement this resource as a prayer service for reconciliation, as a substitute for a sermon, or as an addition to a sermon. In the classroom, the drama by itself can act as a teaching aid to a variety of topics — forgiveness, God's undying love, separation from God, children of God and their inheritance, self-righteousness, brotherly forgiveness.

May God grant all those who engage in this service a glimpse of his deep abiding love.

Maxine Dudley

The Prodigal Son

The following account of the parable of the prodigal son is from Luke 15:11-32.

Then Jesus said, "There was a man who had two sons. The younger of them said to his father, 'Father, give me the share of the property that will belong to me.' So he divided his property between them. A few days later the younger son gathered all he had and traveled to a distant country, and there he squandered his property in dissolute living. When he had spent everything, a severe famine took place throughout that country, and he began to be in need. So he went and hired himself out to one of the citizens of that country, who sent him to his fields to feed the pigs. He would gladly have filled himself with the pods that the pigs were eating; and no one gave him anything. But when he came to himself he said, 'How many of my father's hired hands have bread enough and to spare, but here I am dying of hunger! I will get up and go to my father, and I will say to him, "Father, I have sinned against heaven and before you; I am no longer worthy to be called your son; treat me like one of your hired hands." ' So he set off and went to his father. But while he was still far off, his father saw him and was filled with compassion; he ran and put his arms around him and kissed him. Then the son said to him, 'Father, I have sinned against heaven and before you; I am no longer worthy to be called your son.' But the father said to his slaves, 'Quickly, bring out a robe — the best one — and put it on him; put a ring on his finger and sandals on his feet. And get the fatted calf and kill it, and let us eat and celebrate; for this son of mine was dead and is alive again; he was lost and is found!' And they began to celebrate.

"Now his elder son was in the field; and when he came and approached the house, he heard music and dancing. He called one of the slaves and asked what was going on. He replied, 'Your brother has come, and your father has killed the fatted calf, because he has got him back safe and sound.' Then he became angry and refused to go in. His father came out and began to plead with him. But he answered his father, 'Listen! For all these years I have been working like a slave for you, and I have never disobeyed your command; yet you have never given me even a young goat so that I might celebrate with my friends. But when this son of yours came back, who has devoured your property with prostitutes, you killed the fatted calf for him!' Then the father said to him, 'Son, you are always with me, and all that is mine is yours. But we had to celebrate and rejoice, because this brother of yours was dead and has come to life; he was lost and has been found.' "

The Prodigal Daughter

To Prepare: As the audience enters the church each participant is given half a red paper heart. On one side is written the name Jesus and the other side Father. (See page 18.) Reflective music may be sung as participants enter. When all are seated, the Narrator introduces the service.

Narrator no. 1: To begin our reconciliation service we will have a short play *The Prodigal Daughter.* This drama is taken from the parable "The Prodigal Son" and is adapted to include our Savior, Jesus Christ.

Characters:
>   Mother
>   Sarah, youngest daughter
>   Martha, oldest daughter
>   Clarissa, young model
>   Photographer no. 1
>   Photographer no. 2

Act 1

(The living room of the family home. Mother sits in a chair reading the Bible. Excitedly Sarah enters center stage.)

Sarah: Mom, I've been thinking about my future. I've decided I don't want to go to college. I would like to find a modeling job in New York. But to do this, I will need all the money you have saved for my college education.

(Mother looks at Sarah with concern.)

Mother: Sarah, have you given this some thought? Is this what you really want to do with your life?

Sarah: Yes, it is. All my friends are going to New York to find a job in theater, modeling or art. I want to go with them. I don't want to stay here by myself.

Mother: I would rather you get a traditional education, but I cannot make you stay.

(Mother walks to the safe and removes several thousand dollars and gives it to Sarah.)

Mother: Here, I give you this with love. I will miss you dearly. And I hope that some day you will return home.

(Mother hugs Sarah. Then Sarah leaves stage, counting money. Mother hides head in hands in sorrow. Martha enters with a stack of books.)

Martha: Mom, the great news is I made an A today on my religion test, and I was nominated to run for president of the student council. I am so excited. Mother, you look so sad. Aren't you pleased with my news?

Mother: Oh Martha, your sister has left home to pursue a career in modeling. My heart is broken. I may never see her again.

Martha: Mother, I know you will miss her and I will too. But it will be okay. I'll do my work and her share of the work too. You'll see, it will be okay.

(Martha leaves stage. Mother left on stage head down weeping.)

Act II

(Mother sits on chair in corner of stage with Bible in lap searching for Sarah's return, wiping eyes. On the other side of the stage in the modeling studio Sarah poses while a photographer snaps her picture. Sarah walks to corner, sips a glass of wine.)

Photographer no. 1: Okay Sarah, we will call you if we need you.

(Sarah sits in corner sipping wine.)

Photographer no. 1: Clarissa, are you ready for the next set of photos?

(Clarissa enters with another photographer. Clarissa models clothes, smiling, whirling around. The photographers are going wild.)

Sarah: Don't you need any more pictures of me?

Photographer no. 1: Not right now. We'll call you later. Clarissa is perfect for what we want. See you later, Sarah.

(Photographers and model walk off laughing.)

Sarah: I thought we were friends. Why Clarissa? Why not me?

(Sarah walks off stage and removes her shoes.)

Act III

(While Mother sits on a chair in the corner of the stage waiting for Sarah to return, Martha dusts, sweeps, mops wildly.)

Martha: There is always so much work to be done. Someone has to do it. There I am finished. Now I can study.

(Martha picks up book to study.)

Martha: I am just too tired. I'm going to bed.

(Martha kneels to pray.)

Martha: Dear God, help me never to bring disgrace on my family. Help me always to keep your commandment: Honor your father and mother. Amen.

(Martha leaves. Mother falls asleep in chair with Bible in hand.)

Act IV

(On the other side of the stage in New York City, Sarah is kneeling, begging barefooted with a cup. Clarissa walks by Sarah in an arrogant manner. Sarah pushes her cup toward Clarissa.)

Sarah: Could you spare some loose change for a person in need?

(Clarissa drops a coin in Sarah's cup.)

Sarah: Thank you.

(Sarah watches Clarissa leave the stage.)

Sarah: My life is shattered. I've spent all my money. My fine clothes have been sold. My friends have all left me. I am all alone. I can hardly beg enough money to buy myself a meal.

I wonder what Martha and Mother are doing right now? Probably sitting at the kitchen table talking, laughing and eating.

My God, I am so sorry. I wasn't always like this. There was a time when I was more innocent, more responsible to you and my family. I must find a church.

(Sarah kneels before the cross.)

Sarah: What happened to me? Where did I go wrong? Did I get caught up in the glamour of life? My God there was a time that I knew you. Please don't leave me. I've lost everything. You are all I have left. Are you there? Please forgive me.

(Sarah continues in prayer, head bowed. She wipes the tears from her eyes. Silence for 30 seconds.)

Sarah: I must go home. I am tired. I will tell Mother I was wrong, that I sinned against her and God. And after all I have done I don't deserve to be called her daughter. If she will take me back, I will gladly do all the menial chores just for a roof over my head and food to eat.

Optional — (Sarah dances before the cross to selected music as a prayer of gratitude for being reconciled. When dance ends Sarah walks to front of stage.)

Sarah: I miss my mother!

Act V

(Now outside the family home, Sarah runs across the stage to Mother. They embrace. Mother walks Sarah back to her chair.)

Sarah: Mom, I . . . Mom, I . . . was foolish to be lured by fame and fast living. I wasted all my college savings. Could, could you use some help with the housekeeping?

Mother: I am so glad you are home. I missed you so much. I have wanted you home for so long.

(Mother drapes a fine robe on Sarah.)

Sarah: Mother, this robe is beautiful.

(Mother places a ring on her Sarah's finger, satin slippers on her feet, a wreath of flowers on her head.)

Mother: I just finished this wreath of flowers. Ah, you look so lovely, my Sarah.

(Mother again embraces Sarah.)

Mother: We must rejoice, we must celebrate. My daugh ter is home. I can't wait to tell all the family the good news.

(Mother picks up phone.)

Mother: We're having a party. Can you come?

(Martha enters, holding feather duster. Sarah looks at Martha with joy.)

Sarah: Hi Martha, I've come home.

(Martha walks up to Sarah, fingers robe, glances at Mother.)

Martha: What is this? What is going on here?

Mother: Your sister has come home. We must celebrate with a party. I'm inviting all the family.

Martha: What? After all this time? After all the hurt and pain you have suffered by her silliness. I've been here, studying, keeping your house, cleaning, cooking for you and not once did you give me fine clothing, or jewels, or a party. The commandments say we must honor our father and mother. I have always tried to bring honor to this family. And this is the way I am rewarded, with a party for Sarah?

(Martha throws the feather duster across the stage. Martha stomps to the front of the stage, sits with her back to Mother and Sarah.)

Mother: Martha, don't isolate yourself. Sarah is back, we must celebrate. You must forgive your sister. Your sister who was lost is found.

Martha, my beautiful daughter, everything I have has always been yours. I love you both.

(Silence for 30 seconds.)

Narrator no. 1: The piece of heart you hold represents your separation from the God of Love and his longing for you to return. Only when your heart is united with the heart of Jesus are you whole.

With this symbol of separation in your hands we ask prayerfully for the grace to become aware of our sins, and the grace to grieve for them.

(Silence for one minute.)

Narrator no. 2 *(Representing God the Father):* My child, I will reveal to you the areas of your life that need mending, that are barriers to your loving me. Bring them to me as a child would bring a wound to her father to be healed. As your heart repents, I will give you peace. I will heal your pain, your sorrow. I long to embrace you and turn your darkness to light. I want you to return to me. I love you.

(Silence for one minute)

(Narrator no. 1 leads participants in a prayer of forgiveness or prayerfully reciting an act of contrition. Upon completion of the prayer or act of contrition, the Narrator continues.)

Narrator no. 1: Jesus leads us to the Father's house of love, to your house of love.

Now come forward and place your piece of heart on the altar. Then pick up a whole heart and return to your seat.

(Reflective music may be sung as participants move forward to pick up whole heart. When all participants have returned to their seats, the narrator continues.)

Narrator no. 1: We have given God that which separates us from him. He will give us a new heart which can begin anew, love anew. Then we will be at home with the One who loves us the most.

The following may be used by Roman Catholics:

Narrator no. 1: Those wishing to participate in individual confessions may do so now.

17

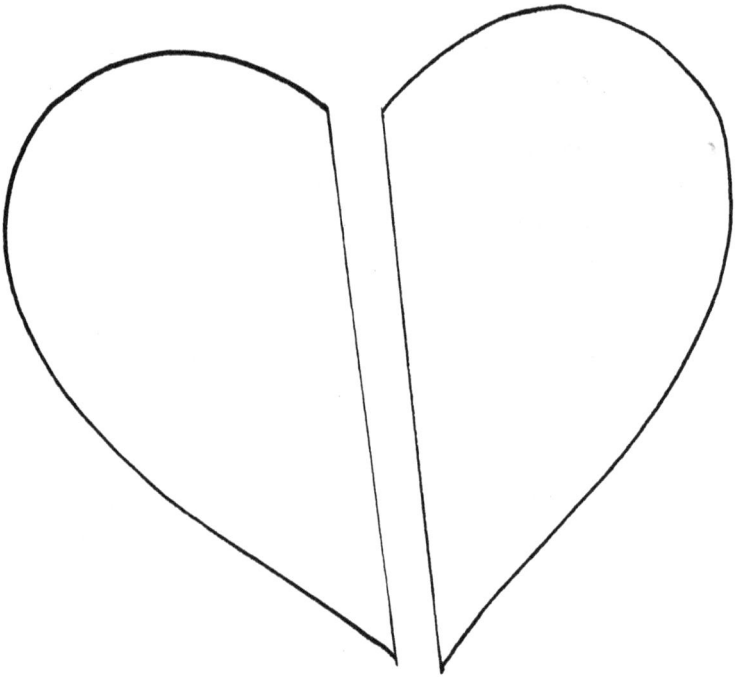

You may use this as a master for your copy machine. See page 9 for instructions. When the hearts are copied, write "Father" on one side and "Jesus" on the other side.

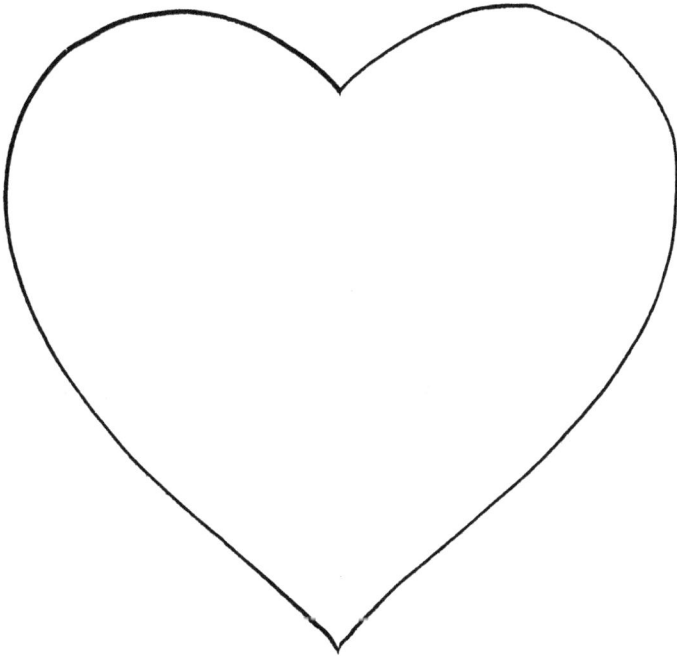

You may use this as a master for your copy machine. It is used on page 17.

www.ingramcontent.com/pod-product-compliance
Lightning Source LLC
Chambersburg PA
CBHW060045040426
42331CB00032B/2490